MW01155254

Instant Pot® Mini Cooking for Two

Beginners Guide with Fast and Tasty Recipes for Your 3-Quart Electric Pressure Cooker

A Cookbook for Instant Pot® MINI Duo Users

Tiffany Shelton

Copyright © 2020 by Tiffany Shelton.

All rights reserved.

No part of this book may be reproduced in any form or by any electronic or mechanical means, except in the case of a brief quotation embodied in articles or reviews, without written permission from its publisher.

Disclaimer

The recipes and information in this book are provided for educational purposes only. Please always consult a licensed professional before making changes to your lifestyle or diet. The author and publisher shall have neither liability nor responsibility to anyone with respect to any loss or damage caused or alleged to be caused directly or indirectly by the information contained in this book. All trademarks and brands within this book are for clarifying purposes only and are owned by the owners themselves, not affiliated with this document.

Images from shutterstock.com

CONTENTS

INTRODUCTION

The Instant Pot Mini Cookbook for Two is a handy guide for busy people who are looking for tasty recipes but aren't ready to waste their time with cooking. With the Instant Pot Mini, it's actually possible!

In chapter 1, you will find helpful information about the key Instant Pot Mini characteristics, including peculiar functions, unique settings for cooking meals from various countries, and the main advantages for busy people of using this kitchen appliance. It can be useful for those who have just purchased such a cool device and are now trying to find out how it works.

The next chapter also contains a lot of beneficial information. From it, you can learn some important tips and hacks that will help you cook with pleasure and avoid basic problems while you're cooking with the Instant Pot Mini.

Finally, you will find more than 50 Instant Pot Mini Recipes for Two in our last chapter. All the recipes gathered in the Instant Pot Mini Cookbook for Two are quite easy and quick, so you don't need to spend most of your precious time cooking.

We tried to select the most delicious recipes that can show you what the Instant Pot Mini is capable of!

CHAPTER 1. Instant Pot Mini - Features & Functions

Main Benefits for Busy People

Today the Instant Pot Mini is one of the most popular kitchen devices. This compact appliance combines a slow cooker, rice cooker, yogurt maker, and, of course, an electric pressure cooker. So how could you not fall in love with such a useful device as an Instant Pot Mini?

Most people who have already bought their Instant Pots Mini can't imagine their lives without this great kitchen machine. There are four main reasons why busy people prefer to use an Instant Pot Mini for their daily cooking routine. These are:

Size

Being a compact kitchen appliance, an Instant Pot Mini can be put anywhere in the kitchen. It isn't difficult to find the right place for such an indispensable device because it actually doesn't take up much space on the counter at all. Besides, mini models are great for small busy families of two.

Price

Instant Pot Mini 3-quart models are known as budget-friendly options, and they don't cost too much. The price for these varies from $60 to $200, depending mostly on the brand and the number of functions. So everyone can select an appropriate model regarding the budget and food habits.

Time-Saving

The Instant Pot Mini can save you not only money but also time. With the Instant Pot, you can cook any meal twice as fast as with other cooking methods. It's the best option for really busy people. In fact, the Instant Pot Mini decreases the consumption rate, cooks dried grains and meat very quickly as well as eliminating harmful micro-organisms in foods.

Functionality

The Instant Pot Mini has a lot of useful and necessary functions. Moreover, the mini model offers more options than any traditional pressure cooker. However, everything depends on the model you've chosen. Most Instant Pots Mini have standard modes such as 'Sauté', 'Pressure Cook', 'Slow Cook', 'Steam', 'Make Rice', and so on. So, think how many kitchen devices you could replace if you put the Instant Pot Mini in your kitchen?

Settings for Cooking Different Cuisines

Are people creatures of habit, especially busy people? Maybe... But not when you have the Instant Pot Mini. This fantastic kitchen appliance offers you a lot of amazing options that let you cook a variety of different meals from various cuisines. And most importantly, the process of cooking isn't too much time and effort. The Instant Pot Mini is always ready to do all the work for you.

Check out Chapter 3 which is filled with the most delicious recipes collected from different countries. In this chapter, you'll find some of the best Italian, Spanish, Indian, Asian, Chinese, and Mexican recipes. Thanks to the multi-functional programmable Instant Pot Mini, you can enjoy a more varied diet and impress your spouse with extraordinary breakfast, lunch, or dinner meals.

Special Instant Pot Options

The Instant Pot Mini is not an old traditional pressure cooker. It is a device full of inbuilt safety features and convenient functions. A large variety of sensors lets you control the internal pressure and temperature. They're designed to enable the Instant Pot Mini to operate within chosen safety limits. Moreover, the sensors allow you to see if the lid is closed or not.

Most Instant Pots Mini offer a standard number of options. Depending on the type of food you're going to cook, you can use different pre-programmed settings.

Pressure Cook

Probably the used most often button on the Instant Pot Mini is 'Pressure/Manual'. This button allows you to regulate the pressure cooker and select the time you want. Just press the '+/-' buttons to control the time, pressure, and temperature.

Sauté

'Sauté' is another often-used button on the Instant Pot Mini. With this excellent function, you can avoid the process of cooking in the skillet or pan. You don't need to use water. You can pour in oil or add another fat to the pot and cook your food as in the pan or skillet.

Bean/Chili

The Instant Pot Mini lets you cook beans and chili very quickly. For example, it usually takes 2-3 hours to cook chili in a slow cooker. But in the Instant Pot Mini, you can cook it within 25 minutes.

Meat/Stew

Cook your favorite meat dishes with the 'Meat/Stew' function. This option can help you get the meat texture you want. Pretty easy and quick!

Slow Cook

The Instant Pot Mini can operate like a slow cooker if you choose the 'Slow Cook' button. It's quite a useful function for those people who like eating stews and really tender meat.

Multigrain

If you like grain meals, you can use the 'Multigrain' button and cook your favorite grains as fast as possible. "Multigrain" is the best option to prepare brown and wild rice in less than 20 minutes.

Porridge

To cook porridge or grains, you can also select 'Porridge'.

Poultry

Chapter 3 contains a lot of chicken recipes. If you like them, you can use the ' Poultry' option to cook chicken on 'High Pressure' for 5 minutes or 'Low Pressure' for 30 minutes.

Rice

It is best to cook white rice, Basmati, and Jasmine rice, short grains, using the 'Rice' function. Choose 'High Pressure' to make the process faster.

Soup

When you want to make broth, stock, or soup, you need to select the 'Soup' button. Here you can adjust the pressure and temperature to speed up or slow down the process.

Steam

The 'Steam' option can replace your microwave oven because it helps you reheat food, steam vegetables, or seafood. Moreover, if you want to make yogurt, don't forget that this process requires two steps. Firstly, you should pour milk into the container and press 'Steam' for 1 minute. Then, let the milk mixture cool down and select 'Yogurt' as usual.

CHAPTER 2. Useful Instant Pot Tips for Success

General Advice

As you know, the Instant Pot Mini can make your life much easier and more comfortable, especially when your work schedule is very, very busy. When using the Instant Pot Mini, you just put all the necessary ingredients in it, choose the right button, press it, and enjoy your tasty meal within minutes. However, if you're going to get the best dishes out of your Instant Pot Mini, there are a few tricks you need to know to make it function better and more productive.

✓ **Use a little liquid when cooking in the Instant Pot Mini**

Remember, your Instant Pot uses steam to create pressure that helps you prepare your meal faster. To build that pressure, the inner pot needs to have at least half a cup of water or any other liquid.

✓ **Don't use just water**

If you want to add some delicious flavor to your meal, it would be better to use flavorful liquids, such as juice, broth, or stock.

✓ **Don't be afraid to use multiple options when cooking**

You don't have to use only one button during a cooking session. Don't forget that the Instant Pot Mini offers you a great variety of options, so why not use it for cooking a real masterpiece of modern cuisine. Look at the collection of our recipes for Instant Pot Mini gathered in

Chapter 3 and pay attention that most of our meals start with the 'Sauté' button and then require other options.

✓ **Regulate the temperature**

Of course, you can select a cooking function with the recommended temperature. But you can control and regulate the temperature by yourself. In such a way, you can actually set up the perfect cooking temperature for whatever meal you're making.

✓ **Add 10-15 minutes to the cooking session**

To create the appropriate pressure, your Instant Pot Mini needs about 10 minutes. Keep that in mind when cooking! If you press the 'Pressure' option, be ready to wait for additional 10-15 minutes to allow the meal adequately pressurize.

✓ **Try not to overcook**

The Instant Pot Mini is a pretty convenient device that cooks foods extremely fast. Read the recipes very carefully and try to follow the instructions closely in order to not overcook dishes.

Basic Troubleshooting Guide

The Instant Pot Mini is considered a safe, versatile, and fast cooking appliance. But that doesn't necessarily mean that it always prepares foods perfectly. Here we've got the list of the most common Instant Pot Mini issues and solutions you need to overcome these problems.

"It takes too much time to start the timer"

As we have said before, the Instant Pot Mini needs time to heat up and build the necessary pressure). So if you read the recipe and it says that the meal will be ready in 5 minutes in the Instant Pot, you have to mentally add 10-15 minutes to that time.

"You see a 'burn' message on the display"

That usually happens if sensors identify that the pot is overheating or in danger of burning the meal. However, you might see this message because there isn't enough liquid in the pot. In this case, you should check out how much liquid you've poured in and if there's not enough, it'll be easy for you to fix this problem.

"You receive a strange code message"

One of the most useful functions is sending error codes to the owners to determine what the problem is with the Instant Pot Mini. In this case, you can look at a list of the codes (on the support page), and find out what has happened to your pot, and solve the problem.

"You hear beeping all the time"

It's quite normal for the Instant Pot Mini to beep. In doing so the pot informs you that it has started or stopped cooking. But if you hear beeping too often during the cooking session, it can be a sign of a problem. Look at the display to see if there's a weird code. In most cases, such frequent beeping is a signal that your meal is overheating.

"My Instant Pot Mini smells bad"

Don't forget that the Instant Pot Mini can absorb different odors easily (especially when you often use pressure cooking). If you like cooking pungent dishes, the Instant Pot ring catches the smells, and they can blend when preparing different foods. Remember this and buy extra sealing rings to replace them if the smell is awful. Besides, be sure that you care for and clean your instant pot properly.

Instant Pot Care & Cleaning

If you have the Instant Pot Mini, of course, you can use it often. However, you need to take care of it in the right way if you don't want to have to buy a new one in a few weeks.

Here are 4 simple steps that help you give your Instant Pot Mini a deep clean.

Step 1: Clean pot exterior housing and rim

You should wet a damp cloth to wipe off any meal residual or stains on your Instant Pot Mini outer housing.

However, it can be quite difficult to clean the rim. That's why it would be better to choose a foam brush to wipe and wash the rim. But if the rim isn't that dirty, you can use a damp cloth to clean it.

Step 2: Wash stainless inner pot

To clean this part of the Instant Pot Mini, you can use warm soapy water. Remember, white vinegar can be useful if you want to remove rainbow or cloudy stains.

Step 3: Wash the lid and Instant Pot parts

After every use, you should rinse the lid under tap water. If needed, you can wash it with warm soapy water by hand. But don't try to wash it in the dishwasher!

Don't forget to wash the Instant Pot Mini parts from time to time. Try to clean the anti-block shield, steam release valve, and condensation collector at least once a week. Just give these pasts a quick rinse, and you will have no problems with your Instant Pot Mini!

Step 4: Clean sealing ring

This Instant Pot part requires thorough cleaning because it absorbs smells very quickly. Firstly, you should gently rinse the sealing ring under tap water. Then, dry it while it's seated in the lid. You can easily remove awful odors out of the sealing ring with the help of white vinegar.

CHAPTER 3. Tasty Instant Pot Recipes for Two

BREAKFAST

Easy Eggplant and Olive Spread

Prep time: 5 minutes

Cooking time: 10 minutes

Servings: 2

NUTRIENTS PER SERVING:

Carbohydrates – 16.8 g

Fat – 11.7 g

Protein – 2 g

Calories – 155.5

INGREDIENTS:

- 2 Tbsp olive oil
- 1 pound eggplant, peeled and sliced
- 2 cloves garlic
- ½ tsp salt
- 1 cup water
- ½ lemon, juiced
- ½ Tbsp tahini
- ¼ cup black olives, pitted
- A few sprigs fresh thyme
- ½ Tbsp fresh extra virgin olive oil

INSTRUCTIONS:

1. Heat the olive oil, add ½ the sliced eggplant and garlic cloves. Cook for 5 minutes.
2. Put in the remaining eggplant, salt, and water. Cook for more 5 minutes.
3. Remove the liquid and add the tahini, lemon juice, black olives, and blend until the mixture is smooth.
4. Put a few olives at the top of your spread and serve.

Boiled Eggs for Lazy People

Prep time: 3 minutes

Cooking time: 3 minutes

Servings: 2

NUTRIENTS PER SERVING:

Carbohydrates – 1.5 g

Fat – 4 g

Protein – 5 g

Calories – 62

INGREDIENTS:

- eggs (you may want more)
- 2 cups water

INSTRUCTIONS:

1. Put a trivet at the bottom of the instant pot insert and pour in 1 cup of water.
2. Place the eggs on the trivet and add the remaining water (perhaps you may need more than 2 cups).
3. Cook for 5 minutes.
4. Peel the eggs, cut, and serve.

Potato Salad

Prep time: 15 minutes

Cooking time: 30 minutes

Servings: 2

NUTRIENTS PER SERVING:

Carbohydrates – 29 g

Fat – 18 g

Protein – 5 g

Calories – 299

INGREDIENTS:

- 6 medium-sized potatoes, peeled and cut into cubes
- 3 tsp unseasoned rice vinegar
- ½ tsp salt
- 2 cups cold water
- 1 large egg, hard-boiled and chopped
- ¼ white onion, finely diced
- 1 stalk celery, diced
- ¼ cup full-fat mayonnaise
- 1 tsp wholegrain mustard
- Black pepper, to taste

INSTRUCTIONS:

1. Pour 2 cups of cold water into your Instant Pot. Add salt and 1 tsp rice vinegar. Put all of the potatoes into the water (add more water if necessary). Choose 'Low Pressure' for 3 minutes and Quick Release. It'll take about 25 minutes to cook the potato cubes.
2. Layer the potato cubes on a tray, sprinkle them with 1 tsp unseasoned rice vinegar, and let them cool.
3. In a separate bowl, mix the mayonnaise, diced onion, celery, egg, and 1 tsp unseasoned rice vinegar. Blend.
4. Add this mixture to your cooled potato cubes and mix one more time.
5. Add some black pepper if you like and serve.

Hearty Steel Cut Oats

Prep time: 5 minutes

Cooking time: 20 minutes

Servings: 2

NUTRIENTS PER SERVING:

Carbohydrates – 50.5 g

Fat – 3 g

Protein – 7 g

Calories – 235

INGREDIENTS:

- 1 cup steel cut oats
- 3 cups water
- 2 bananas, sliced
- 1 cup blueberries, fresh or frozen
- 2 walnuts, out of shells
- ½ cup milk
- 4 tsp pure maple syrup

INSTRUCTIONS:

1. In a pressure bowl, mix the steel cut oats and water. Blend well. Leave it to cook for about 6 minutes on high pressure.
2. Add the blueberries and fill each bowl with 1 cup of oats.
3. Pour 2 Tbsp milk into each bowl and top with banana slices.
4. Sprinkle each portion with 2 tsp maple syrup and serve.

Instant Pot Breakfast Bowl

Prep time: 15 minutes

Cooking time: 35 minutes

Servings: 2

NUTRIENTS PER SERVING:

Carbohydrates – 38.8 g

Fat – 9.8 g

Protein – 52.1 g

Calories – 428

INGREDIENTS:

- 3 tsp extra-virgin olive oil
- ½ Tbsp butter
- ¼ lb bacon, thick-cut
- ¼ yellow onion, finely chopped
- ¼ red bell pepper, finely chopped
- ½ green bell pepper, finely chopped
- 1 clove garlic, minced
- ½ tsp oregano, dried
- Salt and black pepper, to taste
- 6 yellow potatoes, quartered
- 4 cups low-sodium vegetable broth
- ½ Tbsp parsley, freshly chopped
- 2 fried eggs, for servings

INSTRUCTIONS:

1. Choose 'Sauté on medium'. Add oil and butter to the instant pot. Melt the butter and cook crispy bacon slices.

2. Put in the chopped onions and peppers and cook until they're tender.
3. Add the garlic and oregano. Add some salt and pepper. Cook for 1 minute.
4. Put the potato quarters and broth into the pot and mix well. Choose 'Pressure Cook on high' and cook for 12 minutes more.
5. Remove the liquid and Sauté for 2 minutes.
6. Top with fresh parsley and two fried eggs.

Instant Pot King Pancake

Prep time: 10 minutes

Cooking time: 55 minutes

Servings: 2

NUTRIENTS PER SERVING:

Carbohydrates – 59 g

Fat – 3 g

Protein – 12 g

Calories – 320

INGREDIENTS:

- ½ cup all-purpose flour
- ¼cup milk
- 1 egg
- 1 Tbsp granulated sugar
- 1 tsp baking powder
- ½ tsp kosher salt
- Cooking spray
- ½ Tbsp butter, for serving
- Maple syrup, for serving

INSTRUCTIONS:

1. Using a separate bowl, mix your ingredients until you get a smooth mixture.
2. Grease the sides and bottom of your pot with cooking spray and pour your mixture into it.
3. Choose 'Low Pressure' and bake for about 45 minutes.
4. Top with butter and maple syrup and serve.

Breakfast French Toasts

Prep time: 15 minutes

Cooking time: 1 hour 5 minutes

Servings: 2

NUTRIENTS PER SERVING:

Carbohydrates – 54 g

Fat – 15 g

Protein – 16 g

Calories – 411

INGREDIENTS:

- 1 cup water
- 3 eggs
- ½ cup milk
- ¼cup heavy cream
- 2 Tbsp granulated sugar
- 1 tsp vanilla extract
- ½ tsp cinnamon
- ½ tsp kosher salt
- ¼ tsp ground nutmeg
- ½ brioche, cut into cubes
- Powder sugar, for serving
- Maple syrup, for serving
- Cooking spray

INSTRUCTIONS:

1. In a separate bowl, blend the eggs, milk, vanilla, sugar, heavy cream, cinnamon, salt, and nutmeg. Stir in the bread cubes and mix.

2. Grease the dish with cooking spray and pour your mixture into it. Cover with foil and put in the instant pot. Choose 'Pressure Cook on High' and cook for 30 minutes.

3. Top with powdered sugar and maple syrup.

4. Enjoy your meal!

Simple Poached Egg

Prep time: 3 minutes

Cooking time: 6 minutes

Servings: 2

NUTRIENTS PER SERVING:

Carbohydrates – 0.4 g

Fat – 4.8 g

Protein – 6.3 g

Calories – 72

INGREDIENTS:

- 2 eggs
- 1 cup water
- Cooking spray
- 2 silicone molds
- Salt and pepper, to taste

INSTRUCTIONS:

1. Grease the silicone molds with cooking spray and beat the eggs into the molds.
2. Add 1 cup of water into the pot, put a trivet inside, and place the molds in with the cracked eggs.
3. Set 'Pressure Cook on High' and cook for 6 minutes.
4. Add salt and pepper. Serve and enjoy your meal!

Egg Parmesan Muffins for Breakfast

Prep time: 15 minutes

Cooking time: 12 minutes

Servings: 2

NUTRIENTS PER SERVING:

Carbohydrates – 1 g

Fat – 7 g

Protein – 9 g

Calories – 111

INGREDIENTS:

- Cooking spray
- 3 eggs
- ¼ cup milk
- ¼ tsp salt
- ½ cup baby spinach, fresh and chopped
- Black pepper, to taste
- ¼ cup tomatoes, chopped
- 1 scallion white and green parts, chopped
- ½ cup Parmesan cheese, grated
- 1 cup water

INSTRUCTIONS:

1. Grease 2 ovenproof custard cups with cooking spray.

2. In a separate bowl, mix the eggs, milk, pepper, and salt. Whisk thoroughly.
3. Divide the spinach, tomatoes, and scallions into 2 cups. Cover the veggies with the egg mixture. Top with Parmesan.
4. Fill the pot with 1 cup of water, put in the trivet and place the custard cups inside. Select 'Pressure Cook on High' and cook for 6 minutes.
5. Remove the cups and serve.

Morning Cornbread

Prep time: 10 minutes

Cooking time: 35 minutes

Servings: 2

NUTRIENTS PER SERVING:

Carbohydrates – 21 g

Fat – 10 g

Protein – 4 g

Calories – 191

INGREDIENTS:

- 1 cup self-rising cornmeal
- ½ cup self-rising flour
- ½ tsp salt
- 2 Tbsp butter, melted
- 1 Tbsp sugar
- 1 egg
- ½ cup buttermilk
- Cooking spray

INSTRUCTIONS:

1. Put the flour, cornmeal, and salt in a separate bowl and stir well.
2. Add the melted butter and sugar in another bowl. Mix and add the cracked egg and buttermilk. Whisk well again.

3. Combine the flour mix with the egg mixture and blend well.
4. Grease the pan with cooking spray and pour the mixture into it. Top the pan with foil and put it on the trivet (don't forget to add 1 cup of water in the instant pot).
5. Cook the bread for about 35 minutes, selecting 'Pressure Cook on High'.

SIDE & SNACKS

Butter Mushrooms with Garlic

Prep time: 5 minutes

Cooking time: 20 minutes

Servings: 2

NUTRIENTS PER SERVING:

Carbohydrates – 5.1 g

Fat – 16.1 g

Protein – 4 g

Calories – 169.5

INGREDIENTS:

- 2 Tbsp olive oil
- 1 lb small button mushrooms
- 2 Tbsp butter
- 2 tsp garlic, minced
- ½ tsp fresh thyme
- Fresh parsley, chopped
- Salt, to taste

INSTRUCTIONS:

1. Fill the instant pot with olive oil and set to 'Sauté'.
2. Put mushrooms in the pot and cook for about 5 minutes.
3. Add thyme, butter, garlic, and salt. Stir well. Choose 'Pressure Cook on High' and cook for 12-15minutes.
4. Serve with chopped parsley.

Spicy Chicken Taco

Prep time: 20 minutes

Cooking time: 25 minutes

Servings: 2

NUTRIENTS PER SERVING:

Carbohydrates – 27.1 g

Fat – 5.3 g

Protein – 30.7 g

Calories – 277.4

INGREDIENTS:

- 1 chicken breast, boneless, skinless cut into slices
- ¼ (15-oz.) can roasted diced tomatoes
- ½ cup low-sodium chicken broth
- 3 Tbsp hot sauce
- 2 tsp kosher salt
- 1 tsp chili powder
- ½ tsp ground cumin
- ½ tsp garlic powder
- ½ tsp freshly ground black pepper
- ¼ jalapeño, sliced, for serving
- ¼ avocado, diced, for serving
- ¼ red onion, finely sliced, for serving
- 2 corn tortillas, for serving

INSTRUCTIONS:

1. Put the chicken pieces, tomatoes, broth, hot sauce, and spices in the instant pot. Choose 'Pressure Cook on High' for 12 minutes.
2. Put chicken and other fillings into the tortillas and enjoy your snack.

Asian Lettuce Wraps

Prep time: 15 minutes

Cooking time: 3 hours

Servings: 2

NUTRIENTS PER SERVING:

Carbohydrates – 1.3 g

Fat – 14 g

Protein – 33 g

Calories – 502

INGREDIENTS:

- 1 lb ground chicken, cut into small pieces
- 1 clove garlic, minced
- ½ red bell pepper, chopped
- ½ yellow onion, chopped
- 4 Tbsp hoisin sauce
- 1 Tbsp soy sauce
- Salt and black pepper, to taste
- 2 cups water
- ½ can water chestnuts, sliced, drained and rinsed
- 1 cup cooked brown rice
- 2 green onion, chopped
- 2 tsp rice vinegar
- 1 Tbsp sesame oil
- Iceberg lettuce

INSTRUCTIONS:

1. Put the chicken and garlic in the microwave and heat the mixture for about 5-6 minutes. Drain off the extra liquid and put it in the slow cooker.
2. Put bell pepper, onion, hoisin sauce, soy sauce, ½ tsp salt, and ½ tsp pepper. Mix thoroughly. Set on 'Low heat' and cook for 2-3 hours.
3. Mix in the walnut chestnuts, cooked rice, green onions, rice vinegar, sesame oil and continue cooking for 3-5 minutes. Add salt (if needed) and fill two lettuce leaves with chicken filling.

Chicken Burger

Prep time: 5 minutes

Cooking time: 21 minutes

Servings: 2

NUTRIENTS PER SERVING:

Carbohydrates – 16 g

Fat – 18 g

Protein – 32 g

Calories – 368

INGREDIENTS:

- 2 slider buns
- ½ chicken breast, frozen
- 1 cup any BBQ sauce
- 1 cup water

INSTRUCTIONS:

1. Put the chicken breast in the IP filled with 1 cup of water.
2. Use the 'Manual Button' and set to 15 minutes.
3. Slice the chicken breast, sprinkle with your favorite BBQ sauce and serve inside the buns.

Bacon Cheeseburger Dip

Prep time: 5 minutes

Cooking time: 25 minutes

Servings: 6

NUTRIENTS PER SERVING:

Carbohydrates – 7 g

Fat – 40 g

Protein – 19 g

Calories – 471

INGREDIENTS:

- ¼ pound lean ground beef
- 2-3 bacon slices, cut into small pieces
- ¼ (10-oz.) can dice tomatoes with green chili peppers
- 2 oz. cream cheese, cut into cubes
- 2 oz. any cheese, shredded
- 2 Tbsp water

INSTRUCTIONS:

1. Set your instant pot to 'Sauté' and wait until hot. Add the bacon slices and cook until they're browned. Take them out and put on a plate with a paper towel and put aside.
2. Put the beef in the IP and cook for 15 minutes, choosing 'Pressure Cook on High'. Add the bacon slices, diced tomatoes, and cream cheese. Don't mix.
3. Choose the sealing position and cook on high for 5 more minutes.
4. Mix in the shredded cheese.
5. Serve with chips.

POULTRY & MEAT RECIPES

IP Chicken Wings

Prep time: 5 minutes

Cooking time: 25 minutes

Servings: 2

NUTRIENTS PER SERVING:

Carbohydrates – 0.5 g

Fat – 4.4 g

Protein – 5.5 g

Calories –63

INGREDIENTS:

- ½ 3-pound bag chicken wing drummettes
- 2 Tbsp Frank's Red Hot Sauce
- 1 cup water
- 3 tsp any dry BBQ seasoning blend

INSTRUCTIONS:

1. Put chicken wings In a separate bowl. Sprinkle with the hot sauce and 1 tsp of seasoning. Toss well to cover wings.
2. Pour 1 cup of water into the pot and put a rack in it. Put chicken wings on the top of the rack and set to 'Pressure Cook on High' for 10 minutes.
3. Take the wings out of the pot and put them on the baking sheet. Drizzle with your favorite BBQ seasoning blend and toss to cover properly.
4. Broil for 7-8 minutes and serve.

BBQ Baby Back Ribs

Prep time: 10 minutes

Cooking time: 50 minutes

Servings: 2

NUTRIENTS PER SERVING:

Carbohydrates – 18 g

Fat – 9 g

Protein – 14 g

Calories –219

INGREDIENTS:

- ½ rack spare ribs, cut into 2-3 pieces
- 1 tsp kosher salt
- ½ tsp freshly ground black pepper
- 1 cup low-sodium broth
- 3 Tbsp Dijon mustard
- 3 Tbsp packed brown sugar

INSTRUCTIONS:

1. Drizzle the spare ribs with kosher salt and black pepper on both sides.
2. Pour a low-sodium broth into the instant pot and put the steamer insert inside.
3. Layer the ribs on the steamer insert and set to 'Pressure Cook on High' for 25-30 minutes. Simmer for 8-10 minutes.
4. Take the ribs out of the instant pot and stir in the brown sugar and mustard. Put into the pot again and simmer for 6 more minutes.
5. Remove the ribs and serve.

Simple Italian Meatballs

Prep time: 15 minutes

Cooking time: 10 minutes

Servings: 2

NUTRIENTS PER SERVING:

Carbohydrates – 15 g

Fat – 27 g

Protein – 28 g

Calories – 411

INGREDIENTS:

- 3½ lbs ground beef, lean
- ¼ cup onion, grated
- ¼ cup bread crumbs
- 1 egg, beaten
- 1 clove garlic, crunched
- 1 Tbsp milk
- Kosher salt, to taste
- ¼ tsp oregano
- Pinch ground black pepper
- 1½ cup spaghetti sauce
- Fresh parsley, chopped

INSTRUCTIONS:

1. Mix all of the necessary ingredients except the spaghetti sauce in a separate bowl. Stir well and form small balls with your hands.
2. Grease your instant pot with cooking spray and pour the spaghetti sauce into it.
3. Put your meatballs inside and select 'Pressure Cook on High' for 10 minutes.
4. Serve with chopped parsley.

Super-Easy Asian Meatballs

Prep time: 3 minutes

Cooking time: 6 minutes

Servings: 2

NUTRIENTS PER SERVING:

Carbohydrates – 39 g

Fat – 4 g

Protein – 5 g

Calories – 217

INGREDIENTS:

- ½ 28-ounce bag frozen mini meatballs
- ¼ кeduced-sodiumsoy sauce
- 2 cloves garlic, minced
- 1½ Tbsp brown sugar
- 1 tsp sriracha
- ¼ green onion, chopped
- ¼ inch fresh ginger, minced
- 1 cup water
- 1 Tbsp cornstarch
- 1½ Tbsp peanuts, chopped
- 1 tsp sesame seeds

INSTRUCTIONS:

1. Put the soy sauce, garlic, sriracha, ginger, brown sugar, and ½ cup of water in separate. Stir well to combine the ingredients.

2. Put the meatballs into the instant pot. Sprinkle over the sauce and stir to cover the meatballs. Choose 'Pressure Cook on High' and cook for 5 minutes.

3. In another bowl, mix cornstarch and water. Stir thoroughly. Pour the mixture into the instant pot after your meatballs are ready and 'Sauté' for 1 minute more. Top with green onion and serve.

Chinese BBQ Pork

Prep time: 10 minutes

Cooking time: 45 minutes

Servings: 2

NUTRIENTS PER SERVING:

Carbohydrates – 23 g

Fat – 9.4 g

Protein – 36 g

Calories – 326.2

INGREDIENTS:

- 1 pound pork butt meal, cut the longer side into half
- 3 Tbsp honey
- 2 Tbsp light soy sauce
- 1 cup water
- Kosher salt, to taste
- 1 cup Chinese BBQ sauce, for a marinade

INSTRUCTIONS:

1. Pour the Chinese BBQ sauce into a bowl and add the pork slices to marinade from 30 minutes to 2 hours.
2. Pour the BBQ sauce into the instant pot, put marinated pork in the

steamer basket and season with kosher salt. Set 'Pressure Cook on High' and cook for 20 minutes.

3. In another bowl, combine the light soy sauce and honey. Whisk and pour it into the pot.
4. Take the pork out the instant pot and put it into the oven (preheated up to 450 °F). Cook for 4 - 6 minutes on each side until both sides are browned.

Chicken & Broccoli Bowl

Prep time: 15 minutes

Cooking time: 10 minutes

Servings: 2

NUTRIENTS PER SERVING:

Carbohydrates – 8 g

Fat – 23 g

Protein – 22 g

Calories – 387

INGREDIENTS:

- ½ lb chicken breast, cut into small pieces
- Sea salt and black pepper, to taste
- 1 Tbsp olive oil
- 1½ cups broccoli florets
- ½ cup carrot, grated
- ½ Tbsp arrowroot starch
- 3 Tbsp water
- 3 Tbsp low-sodium soy sauce
- 2 tsp oyster sauce
- 2 tsp sesame oil
- ½ tsp coconut sugar
- ¼ tsp fresh ginger, minced
- 1 clove garlic, minced
- ¼ cup chicken broth
- 2 tsp sesame seeds
- ¼ cup green onion, chopped

INSTRUCTIONS:

1. To make a marinade, mix the oyster sauce, soy sauce, sesame oil, coconut sugar, ginger, and garlic. Stir well to combine. Put aside.
2. Sprinkle the chicken pieces with salt, black pepper, and 1 Tbsp of the marinade.
3. Pour the oil into the instant pot and choose 'Sauté'. When the oil is hot, add the chicken and cook for 1-2 minutes. Add the remaining marinade and chicken broth. Choose 'Pressure Cook on High' and cook for 4 minutes.
4. Pour in the arrowroot starch and 2 Tbsp water, the broccoli, and the carrots into the instant pot and sauté for 4-5 minutes.
5. Serve with sesame seeds and green onion.

FISH & SEAFOOD RECIPES

Spicy Shrimp with Feta and Tomatoes

Prep time: 10 minutes

Cooking time: 12 minutes

Servings: 2

NUTRIENTS PER SERVING:

Carbohydrates – 6 g

Fat – 11 g

Protein – 19 g

Calories – 211

INGREDIENTS:

- 1 Tbsp butter
- ½ Tbsp garlic, minced
- ½ tsp red pepper flakes
- 1 small onion, chopped
- ½ (14.5-oz.) can tomatoes, diced
- 1 tsp dried oregano
- 1 tsp salt
- ½ pound frozen shrimp, shelled
- 1 cup Feta cheese, crumbled
- ½ cup black olives, sliced
- ¼ cup parsley, chopped

INSTRUCTIONS:

1. Choose the 'Sauté' function and heat the butter. Add the garlic, red

pepper flakes, onions, tomatoes, salt, and oregano. Cook for 1 more minute. Take tomato broth out of the IP and put it aside.

2. Put the frozen shrimp into the IP and cook for 1 minute, setting to 'Pressure Cook on Low'.

3. Pour in the tomato broth and cook for 2 minutes.

4. Let the shrimp mixture cool slightly. Top with sliced olives, crumbled Feta and parsley. Serve!

Pepper Salmon with Lemon

Prep time: 5 minutes

Cooking time: 10 minutes

Servings: 2

NUTRIENTS PER SERVING:

Carbohydrates – 8 g

Fat – 15 g

Protein – 31 g

Calories –296

INGREDIENTS:

- 1 cup water
- ½ pound salmon filet, skin on
- 2 Tbsp Ghee
- Salt, to taste
- Black pepper, to taste
- ½ lemon, finely sliced
- 1 zucchini, julienned
- 1 red bell pepper, julienned
- 1 carrot, julienned

INSTRUCTIONS:

1. Pour water into the IP and put the salmon skin on the steamer rack. Sprinkle the salmon with Ghee and season with salt and pepper. Top with lemon slices.
2. Turn the IP to the 'Sealing' position and set to 'Steam'. Cook for 3 minutes.
3. Put the julienned veggies in the instant pot, select the 'Sauté' function, and cook for 1-2 minutes.
4. Layer the veggies on the plate. Top them with salmon and lemon pieces.
5. Serve and enjoy your meal.

Salmon with Broccoli and Potatoes

Prep time: 2 minutes

Cooking time: 2 minutes

Servings: 2

NUTRIENTS PER SERVING:

Carbohydrates – 24 g

Fat – 5 g

Protein – 11 g

Calories –177

INGREDIENTS:

- ½ pound salmon filet
- ¼ pound broccoli, cut into bite-sized pieces
- 2 new potatoes, sliced
- 1 Tbsp butter
- Salt and black pepper, to taste
- 1 cup water
- Fresh herbs

INSTRUCTIONS:

1. Pour water into the IP.
2. Season the potato slices, salmon and broccoli with salt and pepper.
3. Layer the broccoli florets on the steamer basket, then put salmon in and top with the potato slices. Spread butter on the potatoes.
4. Set to the 'Steam' function and cook your meal for 2 minutes.
5. Serve with herbs if desired.

IP Steamed Crab Legs

Prep time: 5 minutes

Cooking time: 2 minutes

Servings: 2

NUTRIENTS PER SERVING:

Carbohydrates – 1.2 g

Fat – 16 g

Protein – 12.7 g

Calories –199

INGREDIENTS:

- 1 cup water
- 1 pound frozen king crab legs
- ½ cup lemon juice
- ¼ lemon, sliced
- 3 Tbsp butter, melted
- Parsley

INSTRUCTIONS:

1. Pour water into the IP and put the crab legs on the trivet.
2. Set 'Pressure Cook on High' for 3 minutes.
3. Drizzle the crab legs with lemon juice.
4. Serve with lemon pieces, parsley, and melted butter.

Quickly Steamed Clams

Prep time: 10 minutes

Cooking time: 5 minutes

Servings: 2

NUTRIENTS PER SERVING:

Carbohydrates – 4 g

Fat – 23 g

Protein – 0 g

Calories – 265

INGREDIENTS:

- 2 lb clams, cleaned
- ½ cup white wine
- ¼ cup lemon juice
- 2 Tbsp butter, melted
- 2 cloves garlic, minced
- Salt and black pepper, to taste
- Parsley

INSTRUCTIONS:

1. Put melted butter into the IP, add the garlic, and choose the 'Sauté' function. Cook for 1 minute.
2. Add the white wine and cook for 2 more minutes.
3. Add the clams, lemon juice, and salt. Choose 'Pressure Cook on High' for 2 minutes.
4. Serve with parsley.

IP Mediterranean Cod

Prep time: 8 minutes

Cooking time: 4 minutes

Servings: 2

NUTRIENTS PER SERVING:

Carbohydrates – 0 g

Fat – 10 g

Protein – 14 g

Calories – 140

INGREDIENTS:

- 1½ fresh cod fillets
- 12 cherry tomatoes, washed and diced
- 2 cloves garlic, minced
- 1 yellow pepper, chopped
- 3 Tbsp olive oil
- 1 Tbsp rosemary, minced
- 1 Tbsp oregano, minced
- Salt and black pepper, to taste

INSTRUCTIONS:

1. In a separate bowl combine the diced tomatoes, yellow pepper, garlic, rosemary, and oregano.
2. Add olive oil to the Instant Pot and put in half of your veggies. Choose the 'Sauté' button and cook for 1 minute.
3. Put in the fish fillets and top them with the remaining vegetables.
4. Add salt and pepper.
5. Set to 'Pressure Cook on High' and cook for 3 minutes.
6. Serve immediately.

Mexican Fish Taco

Prep time: 20 minutes

Cooking time: 8 minutes

Servings: 2

NUTRIENTS PER SERVING:

Carbohydrates – 23.2 g

Fat – 10.5 g

Protein – 27.3 g

Calories – 290

INGREDIENTS:

- 1 tilapia fillet
- ½ tsp canola oil
- 1 Tbsp smoked paprika
- 1 Tbsp lemon juice
- 3 cups water
- 2 sprigs fresh cilantro
- Salt, to taste

INSTRUCTIONS:

1. Add water to the Instant Pot and put the rack in.
2. Drizzle the tilapia with canola oil and lime juice. Put into the Instant Pot. Add paprika, salt, and cilantro.
3. Fold your tilapia fillet into the parchment paper and place it in the airtight packet. Put your wrapped tilapia on the rack.
4. Press the 'Manual' function and cook for 8 minutes.
5. Cut the tilapia into the bite-sized pieces and put them on the taco.

Instant Pot Shrimp Mix

Prep time: 15 minutes

Cooking time: 20 minutes

Servings: 2

NUTRIENTS PER SERVING:

Carbohydrates – 18 g

Fat – 33 g

Protein – 22 g

Calories – 438

INGREDIENTS:

- 1 pound baby red potatoes
- ½ sweet onion, chopped
- 2 tsp Old Bay seasoning
- 1 Tbsp hot sauce
- 2 ears corn, cut into large pieces
- 1 pound shrimp, shell-on
- ¼ cup unsalted butter
- 1 clove garlic, minced
- 1 lemon, cut into wedges
- Salt, to taste

INSTRUCTIONS:

1. Put the potatoes, onion, Old Bay seasoning, and hot sauce into the Instant Pot. Top with the corn. Set to the 'Manual' function, choose 'Pressure Cook on High', and cook for 5 minutes.
2. Add the shrimp and cook for 1 more minute.
3. Melt the butter in a pan and add the garlic and salt. Fry for about 1-2 minutes.
4. Sprinkle the butter mixture over your shrimp and serve immediately.

Tasty IP Mussels with Lemon

Prep time: 20 minutes

Cooking time: 5 minutes

Servings: 2

NUTRIENTS PER SERVING:

Carbohydrates – 9 g

Fat – 8 g

Protein – 14 g

Calories – 189

INGREDIENTS:

- 1 Tbsp butter
- 1 shallot, chopped
- 2 cloves garlic, minced
- ½ cup broth
- ½ cup white wine
- 1 lb mussels, cleaned
- ½ lemon, sliced, for serving
- Parsley, for serving

INSTRUCTIONS:

1. Put the chopped shallot and butter into the IP. Choose the 'Sauté' function. Cook for 1 minute.
2. Add the garlic and cook for 1 more minute.
3. Pour in the broth and wine. Select the 'Manual' function for 5 minutes.
4. Serve with lemon slices and parsley.

Simple Instant Pot Shrimp Pasta

Prep time: 5 minutes

Cooking time: 6 minutes

Servings: 2

NUTRIENTS PER SERVING:

Carbohydrates – 76 g

Fat – 9 g

Protein – 25 g

Calories – 501

INGREDIENTS:

- ¼ pound dried spaghetti
- 1 clove garlic, minced
- 1 tsp coconut oil
- 2 cups water
- ½ pound raw jumbo shrimp, peeled and deveined
- ¼ cup light mayonnaise
- ¼ cup Thai sweet chili sauce
- ¼ cup lime juice
- 1 Tbsp Sriracha sauce
- ¼ cup scallions, chopped
- Salt and black pepper, to taste

INSTRUCTIONS:

1. Put the spaghetti, garlic, coconut oil, water, and 1 tsp salt into the Instant Pot. Set to 'Pressure Cook on High' for 4 minutes.
2. In a separate bowl blend the mayonnaise, Thai sweet chili sauce, lime juice, and Sriracha sauce. Whisk well.
3. Mix the sauce mixture into the pasta. Stir in your shrimp and scallions. Choose the 'Sauté' function and wait for 2-3 minutes.
4. Add salt and pepper.
5. Enjoy your meal.

SOUPS

IP Vegetable Soup

Prep time: 5 minutes

Cooking time: 12 minutes

Servings: 2

NUTRIENTS PER SERVING:

Carbohydrates – 17 g

Fat – 1 g

Protein – 6 g

Calories –10

INGREDIENTS:

- ¼ tsp canola oil
- ½ small onion, diced
- ½ Tbsp garlic, minced
- ½ tsp Italian seasoning
- ½ tsp salt
- Black pepper, to taste
- 2 cups vegetable broth
- 2 large potatoes, peeled and chopped
- ½ carrot, peeled and chopped
- 1 rib celery, sliced
- ½ cup fired roasted tomatoes, diced
- ¼ cup fresh green beans, cut in thirds
- ¼ cup parsley, chopped

INSTRUCTIONS:

1. Add the oil to the instant pot and heat it on the 'Sauté' mode. Add the chopped onion and cook for 3 minutes.
2. Add the garlic, Italian seasoning, pepper, and salt. Stir and cook for 1 minute (on residual heat).
3. Pour the vegetable broth into the IP and add the potatoes, tomatoes, carrot, celery, and green beans. Choose 'Pressure Cook on High' and cook for 12 minutes.
4. Top with parsley and add salt and pepper (if required) and serve.

Potato Soup with Cheese and Bacon

Prep time: 15 minutes

Cooking time: 25 minutes

Servings: 2

NUTRIENTS PER SERVING:

Carbohydrates – 10 g

Fat – 4.1 g

Protein – 3.2 g

Calories – 87

INGREDIENTS:

- 1 Tbsp butter
- ½ large onion, chopped
- 1 clove garlic, minced
- ½ tsp fresh thyme leaves
- 3 potatoes, peeled and diced
- 2 cups low-sodium chicken broth
- 1 cup milk, divided
- 1 Tbsp cornstarch
- ¼ cup heavy cream
- Kosher salt and black pepper, to taste
- Cheddar, shredded, for serving
- Cooked bacon, chopped, for serving
- Chives, chopped, for serving

INSTRUCTIONS:

1. Melt the butter in the IP, using the 'Sauté' mode. Add the chopped onion

and wait for 5 minutes. Add the garlic and thyme and cook for 1 more minute.

2. Pour in the broth and put the potatoes into the pot. Set to 'Pressure Cook on High' for 8 minutes.

3. In a separate bowl, mix ½ cup milk and cornstarch. Put aside.

4. Choose the 'Sauté' mode again and pour the milk mixture into it. Add the remaining milk and heavy cream. Let the mixture boil for 5 minutes.

5. Add salt and pepper. Serve!

Low-Calorie Lentil Soup

Prep time: 10 minutes

Cooking time: 30minutes

Servings: 2

NUTRIENTS PER SERVING:

Carbohydrates – 105 g

Fat – 0 g

Protein – 8 g

Calories –128

INGREDIENTS:

- ½ large onion, chopped
- ½ small carrot, peeled and chopped
- 1 stalk celery, chopped
- 1½ cloves garlic, minced
- 1 cup green lentils
- ½ (14.5-oz.) can tomatoes, diced
- 1 tsp fresh thyme
- ½ tsp Italian seasoning
- Kosher salt and black pepper, to taste
- 2 cups vegetable broth
- 2 cup baby spinach

INSTRUCTIONS:

1. Mix the onion, garlic, celery, carrot, lentil, and tomatoes in the instant pot. Add the thyme, Italian seasoning, salt, and pepper. Add the broth and stir well to combine.
2. Choose 'Pressure Cook on High' and cook for 18 minutes.
3. Mix in the spinach and serve.

Instant Pot Soup with Broccoli

Prep time: 5 minutes

Cooking time: 1 minute

Servings: 2

NUTRIENTS PER SERVING:

Carbohydrates – 24 g

Fat – 26 g

Protein – 15 g

Calories – 374

INGREDIENTS:

- 1 Tbsp unsalted butter
- ½ cup onion, diced
- 1 clove garlic, minced
- 1 can (14.5 oz)reduced-sodium chicken broth
- 2 cups broccoli florets, cut in bite-size
- ½ cup carrot, chopped
- ½ tsp salt
- ¼ tsp ground black pepper
- ¼ cup cornstarch
- ¼ cup water

INSTRUCTIONS:

1. Choose the 'Sauté' mode and heat the instant pot. Add the onion and butter. Cook for 3 minutes.
2. Add the garlic and sauté for 1 more minute.
3. Pour in the chicken broth and add the broccoli, carrot, salt, and pepper. Set to 'Pressure Cook on High' and cook for 1 minute.
4. In a separate bowl blend the cornstarch and water. Whisk well and add to the pot. Select 'Sauté' again and wait for 1 minute.
5. Add salt and black pepper if needed and serve.

Curried Carrot Soup

Prep time: 10minutes

Cooking time: 5 minutes

Servings: 2

NUTRIENTS PER SERVING:

Carbohydrates – 25 g

Fat – 2 g

Protein – 3 g

Calories –117

INGREDIENTS:

- 1 Tbsp extra virgin olive oil
- ½ onion, chopped
- ½ pound carrot, peeled and chopped
- 1 clove garlic, minced
- 1 tsp fresh turmeric, grated
- 1 tsp curry powder
- ½ tsp ground cumin
- ½ tsp sea salt
- ½ potato, peeled and diced
- 2 cups vegetable broth
- ½ Tbsp apple juice
- Ground chiles, for serving

INSTRUCTIONS:

1. Pour the oil into the instant pot. Heat it with the 'Sauté' function. Add the onions, carrots, and garlic. Cook for 5 minutes.

2. Mix in the curry powder, turmeric, cumin, and salt. Cook for 1 more minute.
3. Add the vegetable broth, potatoes, and apple juice. Cook for 5 minutes, choosing 'Pressure Cook on High'.
4. Add the salt and pepper. Let the soup cool and make a puree using a blender.
5. Top with ground chiles and serve.

Wild Rice Soup with Creamy Mushrooms

Prep time: 15 minutes

Cooking time: 45 minutes

Servings: 2

NUTRIENTS PER SERVING:

Carbohydrates – 39.7 g

Fat – 13.7 g

Protein – 10.1 g

Calories –313

INGREDIENTS:

- 2 carrots, chopped
- 3 stalks celery, chopped
- ¼ onion, chopped
- 2 cloves garlic, minced
- ½ cup uncooked wild rice
- 4 ounces fresh mushrooms, sliced
- 2 cups vegetable broth
- 1 tsp salt
- 1 tsp poultry seasoning
- ¼ tsp dried thyme
- 3 Tbsp butter
- ¼ cup flour
- 1 cup milk

INSTRUCTIONS:

1. Put in all of the ingredients except the butter, milk, and flour into the IP and cook for 45 minutes. Use the 'Manual/High Pressure'.

2. Use a saucepan to melt the butter and stir in the flour. Pour the milk into the saucepan and whisk until it becomes a smooth sauce.

3. Combine the sauce mixture with the soup.

Tomato Soup with Basil and Parmesan

Prep time: 20minutes

Cooking time: 30 minutes

Servings: 2

NUTRIENTS PER SERVING:

Carbohydrates – 14 g

Fat – 22 g

Protein – 10 g

Calories –297

INGREDIENTS:

- 1 Tbsp olive oil
- ½ cup carrot, chopped
- ½ cup onion, chopped
- ½ cup celery, chopped
- ¼ (14.5-ounce) can diced tomatoes, undrained
- 1 Tbsp tomato paste
- 2 cups low-sodium chicken broth
- ¼ cup fresh basil leaves, chopped
- 4 leaves basil, for serving
- 1 tsp dried oregano leaves
- ¼cup butter, melted
- ¼ cup all-purpose flour
- ½ cup Parmesan cheese, grated
- Salt and black pepper, to taste

INSTRUCTIONS:

1. Pour the oil into the instant pot. Heat it with the 'Sauté' function. Add the

onions, carrots, and celery. Sauté for 2 minutes.
2. Add the diced tomatoes, tomato paste, chicken broth, oregano, and basil. Mix well. Set the valve to the 'Sealing' position and cook on 'High Pressure' for 5 minutes. Whisk the mixture with a blender.
3. Blend the melted butter and flour in a saucepan,. Cook for 10 minutes to make the roux.
4. Add your pureed soup to the roux. Stir well. Put in the grated Parmesan cheese, salt, and pepper.
5. Top with basil leaves and serve.

Instant Pot Noodle Soup with Chicken

Prep time: 10 minutes

Cooking time: 35 minutes

Servings: 2

NUTRIENTS PER SERVING:

Carbohydrates – 29 g

Fat – 7 g

Protein – 24 g

Calories –269

INGREDIENTS:

- 1 Tbsp extra virgin olive oil
- ½ yellow onion, chopped
- 1 carrot, peeled and diced
- 1 stalk celery, chopped
- 1 clove garlic, minced
- 2 tsp fresh thyme leaves
- 1 lb chicken breast, skinless and cut into pieces
- Kosher salt and ground black pepper, to taste
- 2 cups low-sodium chicken broth
- 2 cups cold water
- 4 oz. egg noodles
- 2 Tbsp parsley, chopped, for serving

INSTRUCTIONS:

1. Pour the oil into the instant pot. Heat it with the 'Sauté' function. Add the

onions, carrots, and celery. Cook for 6-8 minutes.

2. Add the thyme and garlic and cook for 1 more minute. Add the chicken breast, salt, and pepper.

3. Pour the broth and water into the pot. Choose the 'Soup' button and cook for 7 minutes. Remove the chicken breast pieces from the pot and add the egg noodles. Choose the 'Sauté' function and cook for 4-6 minutes.

4. Top with chopped parsley and serve.

Quick Salmon Tortellini Soup

Prep time: 5 minutes

Cooking time: 15 minutes

Servings: 2

NUTRIENTS PER SERVING:

Carbohydrates –57.3 g

Fat – 12.9 g

Protein – 18.4 g

Calories – 406

INGREDIENTS:

- ¼ onion, diced
- 2 cloves garlic, minced
- 2 strips bacon, diced
- 12-14 ounces salmon, frozen and boneless, cut into 3-4 pieces
- 1 (10-oz.) package mixed vegetables, mixed
- 6 ounces tortellini, frozen
- 1 quart vegetable broth
- 1 tsp paprika
- 1 tsp Old Bay seasoning (optional)
- 2-3 handfuls fresh baby spinach

INSTRUCTIONS:

1. Put the chopped bacon, garlic, and onion into the pot and choose the 'Sauté' function. Cook for 3 minutes, don't forget to stir.
2. Add the frozen salmon, vegetables, tortellini, vegetable broth, and seasoning to the Instant Pot. Mix well and use the 'Manual' button. Cook your soup for 7 minutes.
3. Add the baby spinach and serve.

GRAINS & RICE RECIPES

Instant Pot Buddha Mix

Prep time: 10 minutes

Cooking time: 25 minutes

Servings: 2

NUTRIENTS PER SERVING:

Carbohydrates – 90 g

Fat – 22 g

Protein – 22 g

Calories – 600

INGREDIENTS:

- ½ cup uncooked grains (rice, barley, millet, etc.)
- 3 cups leafy greens (spinach, kale, cabbage, broccoli, bell pepper, etc.)
- 1 cup cooked legumes (any beans, chickpeas, peas, edamame, etc.)

INSTRUCTIONS:

1. Pour 1 cup of water into the IP and cook the grains on 'Pressure Cook on High' for 20-25 minutes.
2. Chop the greens.
3. Make a tasty dressing.
4. Combine all of the ingredients and mix well.

Rice Bowl with Spanish Chicken

Prep time: 15 minutes

Cooking time: 40 minutes

Servings: 2

NUTRIENTS PER SERVING:

Carbohydrates – 21.4 g

Fat – 17 g

Protein – 23.3 g

Calories –334

INGREDIENTS:

- 2 chicken thighs, boneless and skinless
- 1 pinch salt
- 1 Tbsp olive oil
- 1 red bell pepper, diced
- ½ onion, sliced
- 2 cloves garlic, minced
- 1 tsp ground cumin
- 1 tsp ground red pepper
- 1 tsp dried oregano
- ½ pound tomatoes, diced
- 1 cup chicken broth
- 1 cup long-grain rice
- ½ cup frozen peas, thawed

INSTRUCTIONS:

1. Season each chicken thigh with salt.
2. Heat the olive oil in the IP on 'Sauté and cook the chicken thighs in it for 3 minutes each side. Take them out and put aside.
3. Put the bell pepper, garlic, and onion in the instant pot and sauté for 1 minute. Add the salt, cumin, red pepper, and oregano. Stir well. Cook for 3-5 more minutes.
4. Stir in the tomatoes and chicken broth. Add the rice and return the chicken thighs to the pot. Select 'Pressure Cook on High' and cook for 12 minutes. Add the peas and sauté for 5 minutes.
5. Serve your meal.

Delicious Coconut Rice

Prep time: 2 minutes

Cooking time: 28 minutes

Servings: 2

NUTRIENTS PER SERVING:

Carbohydrates – 38 g

Fat – 12 g

Protein – 4 g

Calories – 280

INGREDIENTS:

- ½ cup Basmati rice, rinsed
- ½ cup coconut milk, unsweetened
- ¼ cup water
- Green onions, chopped

INSTRUCTIONS:

1. Blend the rice, coconut milk, water, and salt with the IP steel insert.
2. Set to the 'Rice' function and cook for 12 minutes on 'Low Pressure' or 4 minutes on 'High Pressure'.
3. Top with the chopped green onion and serve.

IP Lemon Rice

Prep time: 5 minutes

Cooking time: 5 minutes

Servings: 2

NUTRIENTS PER SERVING:

Carbohydrates – 55 g

Fat – 8g

Protein – 7 g

Calories – 332

INGREDIENTS:

- 1 cup Basmati rice, rinsed
- 2 cups water
- ¼ cup lemon juice
- ¼ lemon, thinly sliced

INSTRUCTIONS:

1. Pour the water into the IP, add the rice, and lemon juice.
2. Set to 'High Pressure' and cook the rice for 4-5 minutes.
3. Serve with lemon slices.

Quick Quinoa

Prep time: 1 minute

Cooking time: 20 minutes

Servings: 2

NUTRIENTS PER SERVING:

Carbohydrates – 36 g

Fat – 3 g

Protein – 8 g

Calories – 208

INGREDIENTS:

- 1 cup Quinoa, washed
- 1 cup water

INSTRUCTIONS:

1. Put the quinoa and water into the instant pot.
2. Set to 'High Pressure' and cook for 1 minute.
3. Do a natural pressure release. Fluff with a fork.
4. Serve.

Indian Lentil with Veggies

Prep time: 5 minutes

Cooking time: 20 minutes

Servings: 2

NUTRIENTS PER SERVING:

Carbohydrates – 30 g

Fat – 8.2 g

Protein – 5.2 g

Calories – 208

INGREDIENTS:

- ½ cup split green moong lentils, washed
- ½ cup white rice, rinsed
- 2 cups water
- 1 Tbsp Ghee
- ½ tsp cumin seeds
- ½ Tbsp ginger, paste
- ½ small onion, chopped
- 1 small tomato, chopped
- 1 small potato, cut into cubes
- ½ cup carrot, cut into small pieces
- ½ cup green peas
- Salt, to taste
- Cilantro, for serving

INSTRUCTIONS:

1. Set to 'Sauté' and heat the Ghee in the pot.
2. Add the cumin seeds and cook them for 30 seconds. Add the onion and ginger and cook for 1 more minute.
3. Put all the vegetables, rice, lentils, and spices in the instant pot. Stir well and cook for 5 minutes on 'High Pressure' on the sealing position.
4. Top with cilantro and serve.

DESERTS

Instant Pot Homemade Caramel

Prep time: 5 minutes

Cooking time: 40 minutes

Servings: 2

NUTRIENTS PER SERVING:

Carbohydrates – 32 g

Fat – 5 g

Protein – 5 g

Calories – 191

INGREDIENTS:

- 1 (14-ounce) can sweetened condensed milk
- ½ tsp pure vanilla extract
- 4-5 cups water

INSTRUCTIONS:

1. Fill your instant pot with 4-5 cups of water.
2. Open your condensed milk and wrap it in the foil. Put in the middle of the pot.
3. Set to 'Pressure Cook on High' and cook for 35 minutes.

Mexican Rice Pudding

Prep time: 5 minutes

Cooking time: 30 minutes

Servings: 2

NUTRIENTS PER SERVING:

Carbohydrates – 32 g

Fat – 4 g

Protein – 4 g

Calories – 188

INGREDIENTS:

- 6 Tbsp long-grain rice, rinsed
- 1 cup water
- ½ cup whole milk
- Pinch kosher salt
- 2 Tbsp sweetened condensed milk
- ¼ tsp vanilla extract
- Ground cinnamon

INSTRUCTIONS:

1. Put the rinsed rice, water, milk, and salt into the instant pot and whisk.
2. Choose the ' Porridge' option and cook the mixture for 20 minutes.
3. Add the condensed milk and vanilla extract. Stir well.
4. Top with cinnamon and serve.

Indian Cheesecake for Two

Prep time: 5 minutes

Cooking time: 25 minutes

Servings: 3

NUTRIENTS PER SERVING:

Carbohydrates – 39 g

Fat – 5 g

Protein – 6 g

Calories –206

INGREDIENTS:

- ½ (14-ounce) can sweetened condensed milk
- ½ cup whole milk yogurt
- 1½ Tbsp butter, melted
- 2 cups water

INSTRUCTIONS:

1. Combine the condensed milk and yogurt in a separate bowl. Stir well and pour into 2 ramekins. Don't forget to grease them with melted butter beforehand and cover with foil after putting in the yogurt mixture.

2. Add 2 cups of water into the pot and place the trivet inside.
3. Put the ramekins on the top of the trivet and cook for 25 minutes, choosing 'Pressure Cook on High'.

Sweety Pumpkin Pie

Prep time: 10 minutes

Cooking time: 35 minutes

Servings: 2

NUTRIENTS PER SERVING:

Carbohydrates – 42 g

Fat – 19 g

Protein – 5 g

Calories –247

INGREDIENTS:

- 2 Pecan Sandies cookies, crunched
- 2 Tbsp pecans, toasted and chopped
- 1 Tbsp butter, melted
- 2 Tbsp light brown sugar
- ¼ tsp salt
- 1 tsp pumpkin pie spice
- 1 egg, beaten
- ½ cup pure pumpkin
- ¼ cup evaporated milk

INSTRUCTIONS:

1. Mix the Pecan Sandies cookie crumbs, chopped pecans, and melted butter in a bowl. Put the mixture into the bottom of the pan (previously sprayed with non-stick cooking spray) and put it into the freezer for about 10 minutes.

2. In another bowl, combine the pumpkin pie spice, sugar, and salt. Stir in beaten egg, milk, and pumpkin. Pour this mixture into the frozen pie and cover the pan with foil.

3. Add 1 cup of water to the instant pot, put in the trivet and put your pie onto it. Cook for 35 minutes.

Poached Pears with Cinnamon and Chocolate Sauce

Prep time: 15 minutes

Cooking time: 20 minutes

Servings: 2

NUTRIENTS PER SERVING:

Carbohydrates – 129 g

Fat – 26 g

Protein – 4 g

Calories – 813

INGREDIENTS:

- ½ lemon, cut in half
- 2 cups water
- 1 cup white wine
- 1 cup organic cane sugar
- 2 sticks cinnamon
- 2 pears, ripe but firm, peeled
- 3 ounces bittersweet chocolate
- 3 Tbsp coconut milk
- 1½ Tbsp coconut oil
- 4 tsp maple syrup

INSTRUCTIONS:

1. Put the water, wine, sugar, and cinnamon into the instant pot.
2. Choose 'Sauté' and wait for 2 minutes.

3. Squeeze the lemon halves and pour this juice into the syrup.
4. Dip the pear into the syrup, set to 'Pressure Cook on High', and cook for 3 minutes. After removing the pears let the syrup cool and pour it over the pears.
5. To make the chocolate sauce, you need to take a saucepan, put the coconut oil, coconut milk, and maple syrup in it and heat over medium flame until melted. Then put the chocolate in a separate bowl and cover it with this boiled mixture. Whisk and pour it over the pears.

Instant Pot Raspberry Curd

Prep time: 5 minutes

Cooking time: 11 minutes

Servings: 2

NUTRIENTS PER SERVING:

Carbohydrates – 5 g

Fat – 0 g

Protein – 1 g

Calories – 26

INGREDIENTS:

- 2 cups fresh raspberries
- 2½ Tbsp sugar
- 1 egg, beaten
- 1 Tbsp fresh lemon juice
- 1 Tbsp butter

INSTRUCTIONS:

1. Combine all of the necessary ingredients. Stir well.
2. Put the raspberry mixture into the pot and choose 'Pressure Cook on High'. Cook for 1 minute. Let it release for 5 minutes, blend with a food mill, and put it in the instant pot again. Set to 'Sauté' and wait for 5 minutes.
3. Enjoy your raspberry curd.

Easy Apple Crisp

Prep time: 10 minutes

Cooking time: 5 minutes

Servings: 2

NUTRIENTS PER SERVING:

Carbohydrates – 101 g

Fat – 26 g

Protein – 8 g

Calories – 652

INGREDIENTS:

- ¼ cup all-purpose flour
- ¼ cup old-fashioned rolled oats
- ½ cup light brown sugar, divided into 2 portions
- ½ tsp ground cinnamon, divided into 2 portions
- ½ tsp salt
- 3 Tbsp unsalted butter, cut into small pieces
- 2 apples, chopped into non-big chunks
- 1 Tbsp butter, melted
- ½ Tbsp lemon juice
- ¼ tsp vanilla extract
- 1 cup water

INSTRUCTIONS:

1. Mix the flour, oats, unsalted butter, ¼ cup sugar, ¼ tsp cinnamon, and ¼ tsp salt in a bowl. Stir well until it looks like small crumbs. Put in the fridge for 10 minutes.

2. Grease your pot with non-stick spray and put in the melted butter, lemon juice, vanilla extract, remaining cinnamon, sugar, and salt. Whisk thoroughly. Add the water and the apple chunks to the mixture and cover it with the crumb topping.

3. Choose 'Pressure Cook on High' and cook for 5 minutes.

Whole Wheat Pancake Muffins

Prep time: 1 minute

Cooking time: 5 minutes

Servings: 2

NUTRIENTS PER SERVING:

Carbohydrates – 30 g

Fat – 2 g

Protein – 14 g

Calories – 190

INGREDIENTS:

- 1 cup Kodiak Flapjack and Waffle Mix
- 1 - 2 cups water, depending on what kind of Kodiak mix you prefer
- 2 silicone molds
- Cooking spray

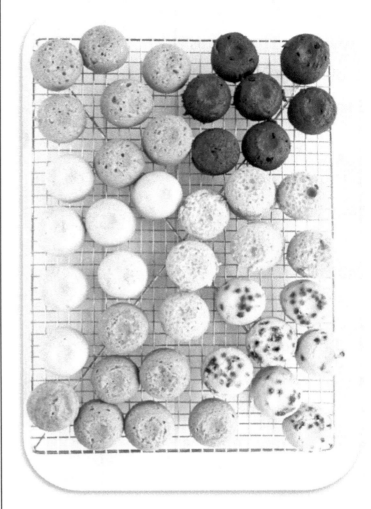

INSTRUCTIONS:

1. Mix the Kodiak mix and water in a separate bowl.
2. Spray the molds with cooking spray and put the batter into the prepared molds.
3. Pour 1-2 cups of water into the pot, put in the trivet and silicone molds.
4. Choose 'Pressure Cook on High' and cook for 5 minutes.
5. Serve your muffins.

Easy Apple Sauce

Prep time: 10 minutes

Cooking time: 4 minutes

Servings: 2

NUTRIENTS PER SERVING:

Carbohydrates – 29 g

Fat – 0 g

Protein – 0 g

Calories – 112

INGREDIENTS:

- 4 big apples, peeled and sliced
- 2 Tbsp brown sugar
- ¼ tsp cinnamon
- ¼ cup apple juice
- ¼ Tbsp lemon juice
- Pinch salt

INSTRUCTIONS:

1. In your pot, blend the apple slices, brown sugar, cinnamon, apple juice, lemon juice, and salt.
2. Choose 'Pressure Cook on High' and wait for 4 minutes. Then set to 'Pressure Cook on Medium' and cook for 10 minutes.
3. Stir the apple mixture using a wooden spoon. If you want a very smooth apple sauce, put the mixture into a food processor and blend for a few minutes.

CONCLUSION

Thank you for reading this book and having the patience to try the recipes.

I do hope that you have had as much enjoyment reading and experimenting with the meals as I have had writing the book.

If you would like to leave a comment, you can do so at the Order section->Digital orders, in your Amazon account.

Stay safe and healthy!

Recipe Index

Conversion Tables

VOLUME EQUIVALENTS (LIQUID)

US STANDARD	US STANDARD (OUNCES)	METRIC
2 tablespoons	1 fl. oz.	30 mL
¼ cup	2 fl. oz.	60 mL
½ cup	4 fl. oz.	120 mL
1 cup	8 fl. oz.	240mL
1½ cups	12 fl. oz.	355 mL
2 cups or 1 pint	16 fl. oz.	475 mL
4 cups or 1 quart	32 fl. oz.	1 L
1 gallon	128 fl. oz.	4 L

OVEN TEMPERATURES

FAHRENHEIT (°F)	CELSIUS (°C) APPROXIMATE
250 °F	120 °C
300 °F	150 °C
325 °F	165 °C
350 °F	180 °C
375 °F	190 °C
400 °F	200 °C
425 °F	220 °C
450 °F	230 °C

VOLUME EQUIVALENTS (LIQUID)

US STANDARD	METRIC (APPROXIMATE)
⅛ teaspoon	0.5 mL
¼ teaspoon	1 mL
½ teaspoon	2 mL
⅔ teaspoon	4 mL
1 teaspoon	5 mL
1 tablespoon	15 mL
¼ cup	59 mL
⅓ cup	79 mL
½ cup	118 mL
⅔ cup	156 mL
¾ cup	177 mL
1 cup	235 mL
2 cups or 1 pint	475 mL
3 cups	700 mL
4 cups or 1 quart	1 L
½ gallon	2 L
1 gallon	4 L

WEIGHT EQUIVALENTS

US STANDARD	METRIC (APPROXIMATE)
½ ounce	15 g
1 ounce	30 g
2 ounces	60 g
4 ounces	115 g
8 ounces	225 g
12 ounces	340 g
16 ounces or 1 pound	455 g

Tiffany Shelton's page on Amazon

CPSIA information can be obtained
at www.ICGtesting.com
Printed in the USA
LVHW061059071021
699818LV00011B/100